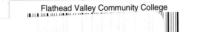

BISON

Symbol of the American West

Michael S. Sample

FALCON®

Helena, Montana

Library of Congress Number 86-82740
ISBN 0-937959-06-5

Published by Falcon® Publishing, Inc.
Helena, Montana. Falcon® publishes
a wide variety of outdoor, history and
nature books. Write Falcon, P.O. Box
1718, Helena, MT 59624, or call toll-free
1-800-582-2665 for a free catalog.

Design, typesetting, and other pre-press work by
Falcon®, Helena, Montana. Printed in Hong Kong.

A dedication: This book is dedicated to all who worked so hard to bring the bison back from the brink of extinction and who continue to professionally manage the species today.

In Pelican Valley, where winter temperatures sometimes drop to -50°F. and deep snow walls off escape routes, bison survive by foraging along the edges of small geothermal areas. Photo by Mary Meagher.

Introducing the American bison

"The buffalo is a timid creature, but brought to bay would fight with ferocity. There were few sights more terrifying to the novice than the spectacle of an old bull at bay. His mighty bulk a quivering mass of active, enraged muscles; the shining horns, the little spikey tail, and the eyes half-hidden beneath the shaggy frontlet, yet gleaming with rage. . . ." —Ernest Thompson Seton

The story of the American bison is a bittersweet tale indeed. Caught in a massive tug-of-war between the forces of nature and the forces of mankind, the majestic creature barely survived.

The history of the bison represents an epic journey through geologic time, as the animal survived and adapted to changes that eradicated other species. Then, late in the 19th century, during the last days of the 200 years man spent "settling the West," wild bison all but disappeared from this country's prairies and mountains. Directly or indirectly, man trimmed a population of 40 or 50 million large animals to a few hundred scattered survivors in only a few years. Ironically, mankind had to mount a similar massive effort to bring the bison back from extinction.

Now, nearly a century later, perhaps 100,000 bison roam prairies and mountains in national parks and other public preserves or graze placidly in scattered private herds throughout the United States. The bison's place in modern America is finally balanced between civilization and wilderness.

The wild West has been tamed, but the bison remains a wild species in many cases. Today, the bison has become a symbol of the American West—the largest and oldest game animal in North America and the vestige of a way of life cherished but not completely understood.

For naturalist William T. Hornaday, the disappearance of the buffalo seemed an inevitable result of the advance of civilization. "To the early pioneers who went forth to carve the way in the wilderness, to wrestle with nature for the necessities of life," Hornaday once wrote, "this valuable animal seemed like a gift direct from the hand of providence."

Whatever the reason, the bison always has been—and still is—a source of inspiration. Throughout history, the species has proved spiritually intriguing, materially useful, and politically obstructive. The saga of the bison has swung like a pendulum between survival in nature and domination by man. □

The dominance hierarchy of the bison becomes increasingly evident as summer—and the rut—begins. Here, two bulls pursue a cow in Yellowstone National Park. Typically, the weaker bull will yield to the dominant bull, but occasionally, if neither will back down, a vicious battle ensues.

The triangular head of this bull is broader than that of a cow. Bulls carry stouter, more evenly curving horns, rough with burrs at the base. They also sport longer beards. Their skulls are so thick they retarded the bullets of hunters on the American frontier. A double layer of bone protects the brain and serves as a shock absorber.

Nature of the beast

"Nothing can be more revolting, more terrific, than a front view of an old bull buffalo. His huge hump, covered with long wool, rising eighteen or twenty inches above his spine; a dense mat of black hair, padding a bullet-proof head; a dirty drunkard, beard, almost sweeping the ground, and his thick, dark horns and sparkling eyes, give him, altogether, the appearance and expression of some fourlegged devil...." —William Marshal Anderson

The image of the bison inspires feelings of genetic timelessness and physical dynamism. In silhouette, the head hangs low, with black horns curving up and in. A blocky, powerful neck accentuates the hump, a mass of bone and muscle that supports the weight of the great head. Long black hair hangs in a "bonnet" at the top of the head. A cape of brown sweeps from the hump through the forequarters. A much shorter pelage covers the slim rear quarters and tail.

As in other cloven-hooved animals, the upper jaw contains no front teeth. The eyes, set far apart, emit a reddish glow. The tongue is blackish, and the ears are buried in the pelage. Black hooves leave a circular print, and the tail is short with a tufted tip. Mature bulls weigh about 1,800 pounds and stand as high as six feet at the hump. Cows typically weigh as much as 1,000 pounds and stand perhaps five feet at the hump.

In motion, bison exhibit tremendous power and surprising speed. Short front legs, front quarters "deep up and down," and hind legs "cut high in the flanks" are designed "to run fast and a long ways"—at least according to many historic accounts. Oldtimers would josh that "the buffalo could eat breakfast in Texas, dinner in Oklahoma, and supper in Kansas." And when stampeding, the buffalo was known to "out wind a good horse and outrun him after one mile."

While the western way of life saw bison and horse compete in speed and endurance, the everyday habits of the bison on the range evoked a more common comparison. One frontier account found the bison to be "rather sluggish, mild, inoffensive, and dull." To some, the bison had a boring daily routine. He would "eat in the morning, late afternoon, and at dusk, chew cud in repose during the day, sleep quietly at night, remindful of the gentle routine of farm cattle."

But the commonly stolid behavior of the bison can be deceptive. This beast with an apparently peaceful demeanor can leap or bust through a six-foot fence if it chooses. When migrating, it can ford ice-choked rivers during the spring break-up. And during the rut, one-ton bulls

The bison is the largest land mammal in North America, with mature bulls weighing about 1,800 pounds and standing as high as six feet at the hump. A hallmark of the bison, the hump is a feature of the spine, supported by elongated extensions of the vertebrae. The hump could be likened to a giant crane, giving bison more leverage, especially for snow plowing. Dr. Mary Meagher theorizes that some Yellowstone Park bison have unusually large humps because, for several months of the year, they must plow through deep snow to reach grass. Because of their large humps, bison cannot roll entirely over from one side to the other.

smash heads brutally in a way decidedly unlike the average milk cow.

The bison has an acute sense of smell, which it uses in preference to vision and hearing. Historical accounts credit the bison with the ability to distinguish a horse with rider from a riderless horse from as far as a mile away. Even though, as early naturalists noted, the bison could detect the faint sound of a twig crackling underfoot from a distance of 500 feet, the animal would seldom flee unless it caught the scent of danger. The bison is also curious, often pausing after a first dash away to turn and face the source of the disturbance. □

What's in a name?

Yes, the ''bison'' and the ''buffalo'' are the same critter.

Actually, bison is the scientific name for buffalo. The bison is a member of the bos family, related to bovines such as domestic cattle, but distinct from the true buffalo, those of Asia and Africa.

The term buffalo was first used by English settlers. It was a modification of the name *''les boeufs,''* which early French explorers gave to oxen or beef cattle. The first Spanish explorers referred to bison as cattle, using such names as *''vacas de tierra,''* or cows of the country. Usage of the term buffalo, evolving through variations such as ''boffle,'' ''buffler,'' and ''buffilo,'' became predominant about 1845.

During rutting season, a dominant bull warns challengers by swinging his horns, bellowing, snorting, and pawing.

If the would-be usurper remains undaunted, the bulls clash head-on. Each animal struggles to keep his opponent's head between his horns, because slipping away would expose him to horning from the side and sure defeat, if not death. During confrontations such as this one, on page 11, at Wind Cave National Park, bulls have thrown their competitors several feet.

The great herds

"Early in spring, . . . the horizon would begin to be dotted with buffalo, single, or in groups of two and three, forerunners of the coming herd. Thicker and thicker, and in larger groups they come, until by the time the grass is well up, the whole vast landscape appears a mass of buffalo, some individuals feeding, others lying down, but the herd moving slowly, moving constantly to the northward. . . . Some years, as in 1871, the buffalo appeared to move northward in one immense column, often times from twenty to fifty miles in width, and of unknown depth from front to rear." —Colonel Richard Irving Dodge

The Great Plains nurtured the great herds. Naturalists will always marvel at the sheer mass of the "endless" herds of bison.

But bison were, nevertheless, at the mercy of the natural elements. Harsh winters, drought, and fire not only trimmed the herds but changed behavior patterns. Bison established traditional ranges and routes to reach those ranges—usually, but not always, returning year after year to selected winter ranges. When the herds failed to return—disasters aptly noted by Indian and white hunters alike—it caused human hardship, as a source of winter food unexpectedly disappeared.

The bison is a gregarious animal, forming strong bonds with other members of its herd. The size of the herds varies, primarily with the season, reflecting the rut or the winter-range requirements. The herds placidly graze a wide area, traveling in a daily radius of one or two miles or farther, depending on the proximity of water. A stampede could, of course, rapidly increase the radius.

From late fall to spring, bison separate into cow-calf and older-bull groups. The two types of herds intermingle throughout the year, drifting together for a time, and then splitting again.

Dominance, not territory, rules the bison society. Older bulls usually lead bull groups, while mature cows head cow-calf groups. The leaders exercise only a loose control that is most evident when the herd is on the move. During the rut, the two groups stay together for most of the summer, with cows leading the mixed herds as often as bulls.

Leadership of bison herds takes several forms. During severe disturbances, a single animal may initiate movement at the front of the entire group by heading in one direction at a steady walk. During mass group movements, such as grazing, the herd often will move without an obvious

The great bison herds of the nineteenth century ranged onto the open plains to graze during warmer months, then moved back to rough, broken country for shelter during the winter.

leader. Dominant animals may even be positioned in the center or rear of the group, imperceptibly directing travel by shoving and butting other members of the herd before them. Any mature animal might lead a stampede.

The gregarious nature of the bison can lead to a spectacular show of force during stampedes. In addition to real danger, subtle sounds—the snapping of a twig, another animal bounding through high brush, or a close swoop from a flock of migrating birds—can trigger a stampede. And rather than charging wildly and aimlessly, the stampede usually heads for a protected destination, such as a stand of trees or a secluded meadow, to escape the danger, real or perceived.

A stampede may start without any apparent fuss or clamor. A startled buffalo or a wary group spooks, then randomly closes on the flanks of a nearby group, which in turn stirs, creating a chain reaction. The placid, uncoordinated grazing groups transform into a large, rushing mass.

The stampede may end after only a brief dash. But if the stampede continues, the first animals to bolt may get locked into their place at the front, unable to get out of the way as the rolling mass crushes all obstacles. Indian hunters knew that in a confined space, such as the V-shaped stone chutes leading to the cliffs of the buffalo jumps, or *pishkuns,* there could be no stopping the animals.

The monstrous stampedes captured in historical art probably were the result of prairie fire, severe weather, or even a noisy approach by hunters. But the spectacle of a stampede that runs over anything and everything in its way is not the exclusive domain of yesteryear. Naturalist Tom McHugh has witnessed a "directionless...aimless" stampede of about 150 buffalo on the National Bison Range in Montana. When a hailstorm covered the ground with stones as large as marbles, the herd quickly massed and repeatedly galloped in tight, quarter-mile circles. □

A bull, a yearling, two cows and their calves ford Mission Creek on the National Bison Range in Montana. Although cows and calves generally band together separate from the bulls, the two sexes mingle during summer and the rut. Herds also mingle at these times, creating the huge droves so common to historical accounts.

The year of the bison

"If undisturbed, the buffalo frequently graze for days in the same vicinity, moving once each day, usually at evening toward the water. At this time it is a picturesque sight to see them; each band is being led by its chief, and the whole herd by a leader. Flankers are thrown out; the cows and calves are in the center of the herd, which moves slowly. . . .Their heads are down, frequently so low that the long, matted beard drags and brushes the ground." —Theodore R. Davis

With the onset of winter, after the rigors of the rut in summer and early fall, bison spend more and more time grazing, sometimes forsaking the walk to water by eating snow. Little time is devoted to the scratching, napping, and rolling so popular in warmer months. The cow-calf groups (ranging from 20 to 70 animals) and the smaller bull groups (5 to 20 animals) seek bare ground for feeding and standing.

In winter, bison feed on exposed grass, clipping it down to near the level of the snow. In deeper snow, the bison use their necks, heads and horns, swinging from side to side to push snow away and then shoving deeper with their noses to clear a trench down to the feed. Using this method, bison can feed in snow four feet deep.

Bison have a remarkable ability to withstand extreme winter weather. Their thick coats and layers of fat provide ample insulation. Herds generally move into the wind to avoid suffocating in the drifting snow that piles up against any shelter. In a blizzard, bison huddle together for warmth.

The pelage molt occurs in late winter or early spring, as the bison moves off its winter range. The new growth is short, stiff, and dark brown. Tattered patches of bleached winter hair may cling to the capes and pantaloons on the forequarters into the summer, at times creating an almost grotesque appearance.

The rut begins as early as the end of June and continues into September. As bulls pursue cows, the dominance hierarchy of the herd becomes increasingly evident. It is established either passively or aggressively. Passive dominance does not involve any obvious force or threat. The dominant bull approaches other bulls, which move away. Aggression occurs when one bull challenges another which, in turn, refuses to back down.

A bull may signal his intent merely by looking toward

Bison express themselves vocally in a variety of ways, including loud, short sneezes, belching snorts, or bellow-like grunts. The bellowing takes place chiefly during the rut.

the challenger. Sometimes that is enough to discourage the contender. Swinging his horns toward the challenger means the action is getting more serious and sometimes results in mild contact.

If these calmer warnings don't work, the bull or his challenger may begin bellowing, snorting, pawing, rolling in a wallow, or prancing and shaking his pantaloons. If threats such as short charges or shaking the head do not resolve the conflict, a vicious battle may ensue. The bulls charge and collide, head to head. The noisy, dusty contest continues until one bull backs down.

As the dominance hierarchy among the bulls is established, cows and bulls begin the tending bond, in which the bull stays alongside or behind a cow at a close distance, perhaps one to five feet, and sometimes touching. Tending pairs usually occupy the edges of the bison group,

without actually separating from the herd.

Typically, weaker bulls yield the tending bond to dominant bulls without actual physical contact. After yielding, bulls often seek out wallowing areas, pounding and rolling on the mostly bare ground to work out their frustration.

At the end of the rut, the bison herd separates into cow-calf and bull groups. They travel to winter ranges. The pelage thickens once again, ready for the harshness of winter. The year of the bison starts anew. □

Bison are ruminants, or cud-chewers, with a four-compartment stomach characteristic of bovines. Sedges, tufted plants resembling grasses, may provide the margin of survival for bison in the winter.

(Far left) Bulls and cows living in natural settings commonly have a lifespan of 12 to 15 years, but they may live almost twice as long. An exceptionally hardy animal may live 40 years or more.

In late fall and early winter, the bison develops a rich, full, dark brown coat in preparation for the coming cold. The bison is doubly protected: Its brown, wooly underfur is covered by a layer of coarse guard hairs. The color of the coat fades to light brown toward the end of winter, especially among bulls.

Bison prove their durability by surviving -50°F temperatures in places such as Pelican Valley in Yellowstone National Park where no other ungulates stay the winter. In the face of chilling temperatures and deep snow, the bison draws upon its Pleistocene heritage to tough it out until spring.

Whence came the bison

*"The Rocky Mountains would have been hard to reach with
out him . . . he was one of natures bigest gift and this
country owes him thanks . . . ." —Charles M. Russell*

Apparently, the ancestors of the modern bison developed in the "cradle" of mammalian life in central Asia. Then, thousands of years ago, during an Ice Age that dropped the level of the Pacific Ocean more than 100 feet, the relatives of today's species crossed the Bering Strait Land Bridge to what is now Alaska and spread south across North America.

Scientists who have studied the fossil records have not arrived at a consensus on how bison evolved from the early Pleistocene to the modern form. Over time, more than a dozen subspecies of bison lived in concert with the ebb and flow of the four most recent ice ages. Most of these early bison were much larger than modern bison, and the size continued to increase as the descendants of the early bison moved southward into the grasslands of North America.

Bison priscus probably began the direct ancestral line of modern bison. Known as the "steppe" bison, *priscus* crossed into Alaska from Siberia and stayed primarily in the far northern parts of North America.

Apparently, *priscus* evolved into *bison latifrons,* the largest of all bison with horns spanning more than six feet from tip to tip and a body probably twice as large as that of its modern counterpart. *Latifrons* ranged widely to the south, especially east of the Rockies from Alberta to Texas, but became extinct during a period when the climate warmed about 25,000 years ago.

Bison antiquus, a smaller form of bison, possibly a descendant of *latifrons,* extended the range of the bison to the middle and lower portions of North America. *Antiquus* was especially common in today's southwestern United States and in Mexico. Early man hunted *antiquus* until the species disappeared between 9,000 and 11,000 years ago.

Bison occidentalis appeared about 13,000 years ago.

Bison once roamed widely from Alaska and western Canada across the United States and into northern Mexico. These historic herds were believed to have numbered between 30 million and 200 million animals.

Although smaller than *latifrons* and *priscus, occidentalis* had in common with these two subspecies horns which grew back at an angle from the mid-line of the skull. In earlier bison, the horns pointed forward, in more cattle-like fashion.

Occidentalis moved southward, perhaps interbreeding with and eventually succeeding *antiquus.* The two subspecies living in North America today, the plains bison (*bison bison*) and the wood or mountain bison (*bison athabascae*), developed from the lineage of *occidentalis.* The modern European wisent (*Bison bonasus*), may have developed from *priscus.*

Ten thousand years ago, the climate began warming and the glaciers started receding from the Mississippi Valley.

Southern grasslands turned to desert. Bison descended from *occidentalis antiques* lineage, very similar to today's species, moved from northern and southern latitudes to the Great Plains. Eventually their range extended from the Pacific mountain ranges, over the Rocky Mountains, across the Mississippi, and into the Ohio Valley, Kentucky, Tennessee, Virginia, and the Carolinas.

Curiously, at the end of the last age, many large mammals of North America vanished in what is called the "megafauna extinctions." Gone were about 300 species, including the woolly mammoth, saber-toothed tiger, dire wolf, giant beaver, and several species of horse. One fascinating theory suggests that early man's hunting pressure caused the extinctions of

The wisent, the third bison

The European wisent, *Bison bonasus,* is the other living species of bison.

In appearance, the wisent differs markedly from the plains or wood bison of North America. It looks more like an ox, with a smaller head carried higher than that of the American bison. The wisent's hump is less massive and lengthy, the body and legs longer, and the body mass slighter with less imposing forequarters, but larger hindquarters. The wisent's coat is less shaggy, and the tail is longer.

Approximately 1,000 wisents live in preserves in the Bialoweza Forest of Poland and Russia, as well as the Caucasus Mountains of Russia. The

wisent was almost hunted out of existence between 1918 and 1927, but conservationists have saved the species on preserves.

For several weeks after birth, calves remain close to their mothers. After about a month, they gravitate toward "play groups" with other calves and spend increasing amounts of time away from the cows. Calves nurse for about 8 to 12 months. In mid-winter the cow-calf bond begins to weaken.

When abundant year-round forage is available, cows calve every year. But when food is scarce and cows must expend greater amounts of energy just to survive, calves are often born every other year.

Calves share the status of their mothers until the cow-calf bond breaks. Then the youngsters become the most subordinate in the herd.

some of those species which could not adapt or biologically compensate for the intelligent human beings and their increasingly efficient methods of hunting.

But the bison survived. Actually, it did more than that. It prospered. Somewhere between 30 and 60 million roamed the range when European explorers arrived in North America.☐

Most bison die from an accumulation of stress over their lifetimes, not from predation or disease. But wolves in northern Canada often successfully prey on bison. Don Huisman, a biologist at Wood Buffalo National Park, reported seeing three separate packs of wolves kill three bison while he made one airplane flight over the park.

Occasionally a grizzly will approach a lone adult bison to "test" it, but the bear will not attack unless it discerns the animal is injured or sickly.

This bison skull serves as a reminder of the days when bison roamed what is currently called the Pawnee National Grasslands in Colorado.

Photo by W. Perry Conway

The mysterious wood bison

Early-day explorers of the Rockies reported sightings of mysterious "mountain bison," larger, darker and more reclusive than plains bison. Seldom seen, these animals lived, according to the reports, in the western forests and mountains at high elevations.

Some early naturalists thought these mountain bison were actually a southern population of the wood bison known to exist in northern Canada. A few people thought the mountain bison was a distinct subspecies. But scientists, who use such measures as skull and horn sizes to determine whether an animal is a separate subspecies, had little evidence to go on. Most of the bison of the Rockies disappeared 40 years earlier than the great herds of plains bison. Even the wild herd in Yellowstone National Park had dwindled to only a few remote survivors.

The confusion lasted for a long time. After plains bison were transplanted into Yellowstone National Park and later interbred with the native herd, many writers bemoaned the loss of the pureblood strain. But in fact, scientists now believe that the wood bison never ventured south of the boreal woods of northern Canada. Current thinking holds that Yellowstone's "mountain bison" were simply plains bison which, in much smaller numbers, found a niche to their liking at higher elevations. Perhaps because of especially nutritious food, Yellowstone's native bison were, indeed, slightly larger than the average plains bison, but this does not, in the eyes of the scientist, make for a separate subspecies.

Typical wood bison bulls display a longer neck, more rectangular body and a shorter beard than a plains bison. Photo by Terry Hammell/ Environment Parks, Canada.

The changing hunt

"These Indians subsist entirely on cattle [bison], for they neither plant nor harvest maize. With the skins they build their houses; with the skins they clothe and shoe themselves; from the skins they make robes and also obtain wool. From the sinew they make thread, with which they sew their clothing and likewise their tents. From the bones they shape awls, and the dung they use for firewood, since there is no other fuel in all that land. The bladders serve as jugs and drinking vessels. They sustain themselves on the flesh of the animals, eating it slightly roasted. They eat raw fat without warming it, and drink the blood just as it comes from the cattle. They have no other food." —Francisco de Coronado

The relationship between bison and man began in prehistoric times. Early man hunted bison and patterned their life and culture around the materials and images provided by the most plentiful large animal of the American grasslands.

On the Great Plains, Indian tribes moved their villages along the fringes of the bison herds, depending on the animal for their subsistence. As bison moved onto the open plains during the temperate months and then retreated back to broken, sheltered valleys and wooded areas in winter, the Indians followed, altering their hunting methods to match the terrain.

One early technique required Indians to approach the great herds on foot, under camouflage, and carrying bow and arrows, lances, and clubs. Another method called the "surround" had hunters encircling a herd of bison, then running afoot to slowly close the circle, all the while frightening the animals with shouting noises and flapping robes. When the surround had tightened enough to bring the prey within shooting distance, the Indians loosed their arrows and lances, bringing down the bison at the outer edges of the herd.

Also common was the "pound," a technique used for hunting in wooded areas. Indians built corralled enclosures with six-or-eight-foot high piles of rocks, wood, and brush, chased bison into the traps, and then used their weapons to kill the animals at close quarters.

But perhaps the most glorified method was the use of the "buffalo jump" or *pishkun*. Hunters stampeded herds of bison over cliffs or bluffs up to 250 feet high, at the foot of which was a corral or pen to trap and finish off with clubs, spears, knives, and arrows the frenzied bison not killed in the leap. Buffalo jumps were located near areas where the herds frequently grazed. When the Indians found a good runway to a cliff, they rolled boulders or piled small stones at intervals leading to it. The Indians crouched behind the

Hayden Valley, in Yellowstone National Park, is a historical summer range of the bison. Re-established in 1936, today the herd numbers 1,000 to 1,200 animals.

stones, then popped up and startled the bison into stampeding over the precipice.

The Indians usually used every part of the bison for their material and spiritual needs. At times Indians did overhunt, killing thousands in a single foray. Running the bison over the jumps often resulted in overkill. At other times, when the bison wandered to unknown ranges, Indians faced starvation.

The importance of the bison in the lives of the early hunters can hardly be overstated. It was a central feature of Indian culture. The Plains Indians wove the material importance of the bison into their spiritual beliefs and ceremonies. Some tribes called the bison "Besha," or the great heaven-sent source of most of the necessities of life. The Crow Indians' word for the bison bull was "cherapa," the word of reverence. Other tribes attributed special qualities to this essential animal, such as an ability to emanate from beneath the ground.

Around 1700, the horse became part of the Indian culture and helped tribes not only to extend the range of their nomadic life, but to increase success in hunting. In the 1870s, after the Plains Indians had been taming horses for almost two centuries, they embraced the repeating rifle as a hunting weapon. The rifle displaced the bow and arrow and also improved the Indians' ability to kill bison.

Even with these changes in Indian hunting methods and weapons, the enormous herds of plains bison were never threatened with extinction. However, the bison that inhabited the Rocky Mountains and extended into the Columbian plateau of the Pacific Northwest were less numerous. A combination of severe winters and heavy hunting by Indians nearly exterminated them before 1800.

Thus, a classic period for the Plains Indian began in

Once running, a bison will trample anything in its path, including other bison too slow to keep up. This mad rush enabled early Indians to hunt the animal by stampeding it over pishkuns, *or buffalo jumps, such as this one in Montana. Researchers found bone debris 60 inches deep in places below this buffalo jump, which was used at least 2,000 years ago up until the time horses became widely available to the Native Americans.*

about 1700 with the introduction of the horse and came to an end in the late 1800s. The settlement of the West by the white man doomed both the free-ranging bison herds and the nomadic life of the Plains Indians.☐

The buffalo nickel

Befitting David Dary's words in *The Buffalo Book* that, "Perhaps no animal in the history of any nation has ever played a more important role than the American buffalo," the visage of the buffalo adorns numerous objects and institutions. As a symbol, the buffalo has also been prominent on both currency and coin.

In 1901 the U.S. Treasury issued a $10 note, the so-called "Buffalo-bill." In 1913, the buffalo nickel replaced the Lincoln nickel. Its designer, James Earle Fraser, found no motif as distinctively American as the buffalo. But naturalist William T. Hornaday decried the coin upon first inspection, calling it "a sad failure as a work of art. The buffalo head droops and it looks as if it had spent its life in a small enclosure."

The tool of extinction

"[Buffalo hunters] have done in the last two years and will do more in the next year to settle the vexed Indian question, than the entire regular army has done in the last thirty years. They are destroying the Indian's commissary, and it is a well-known fact that an army losing its base of supplies is placed at a great disadvantage. Send them powder and lead, if you will; for the sake of a lasting peace, let them kill, skin and sell until the buffaloes are exterminated." —General Philip Sheridan

The hunting habits of Native Americans and white hunters did not differ substantially. It was more a matter of degree. Both hunted and killed bison, often taking more animals than necessary. But only the white hunters exerted such pressure that they jeopardized the existence of an unbelievably abundant species.

The bison population was, incidentally, already on its way down. Naturalist Ernest Thompson Seton once postulated,

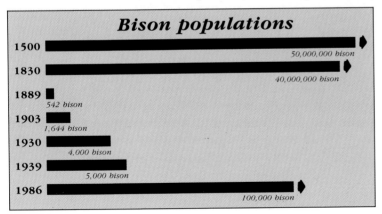

Bison populations

1500	50,000,000 bison
1830	40,000,000 bison
1889	542 bison
1903	1,644 bison
1930	4,000 bison
1939	5,000 bison
1986	100,000 bison

for example, that the population shrank from 60 million to 30 million between 1500 and 1800. But by the year 1895, Seton had to severely revise his estimate, as he then thought only 800 buffalo remained alive in the United States.

The story has been told and re-told, and it is always depressing.

Although the fur trade had existed since about 1764, the development of a commercial process for "tanning" leather hides did not occur until the 1860s. Where previously an Indian woman could prepare perhaps ten robes for the market in one season, buffalo hunters employing skinners could now fill their hunting camps with thousands upon thousands of hides for shipment to the tanning factories of the East.

In the 1870s, the invention of refrigerated railroad cars increased the distance hides could be shipped. Buffalo robes, along with select cuts of buffalo meat, principally the tongue, came into vogue.

In 1867, the extension of the Union Pacific Railroad from Nebraska into Wyoming divided the northern and south-

The great herds are gone, of course, but small herds such as this one on the National Bison Range in Montana have a secure future.

ern bison herds. Then, with the building of the Atchison, Topeka & Santa Fe line through Kansas and Colorado and the extension of the Northern Pacific line from Bismarck, North Dakota, into Montana, the means were at hand to finish the hunt.

The demand for buffalo meat and robes was soaring. Miners, ranchers and farmers were settling the West. The demise of the bison obviously meant the demise of the Plains Indian, so the military encouraged the slaughter as a means to win the Indian wars. All this created the conditions in which the great herds would nearly disappear within a geological second, a mere 25 years.

By 1840, bison already had disappeared east of the Mississippi River. Then, the assault on the central plains began.

The campaign didn't really get serious until the mid-1870s, with the war centered in the southern plains. The southern herds were gone by the late 1870s. Finally, in the early 1880s, the buffalo hunters turned to the northern herds with "victory" in sight, even though those herds still numbered about 6 million animals.

The last battle did not take long. By about 1883, the great hunt was over. The great herds were gone.

A few hundred scattered survivors remained. Luckily they were missed, for they provided the seed for a classic comeback. □

In the early morning mist, the young bull and cow on the right watch warily as a mature bull keeps his "tended" cow separated from the herd.

A mature bull waits out a Yellowstone Park winter.

Buffalo Bill

William F. Cody parlayed a notable career as a buffalo hunter into a flamboyant stage show that gave the world its exaggerated image of the Wild West.

Before he was 21, Cody rode with the Pony Express, distinguishing himself as a rider of courage and endurance. He completed the third longest emergency ride in the history of the Pony Express. In the early years of the Civil War, he served with Kansas militias.

Cody earned his nickname only in part because of his hunting prowess. In the fall of 1867, the Union Pacific Railroad hired him to help feed construction crews. Working alone, he killed, skinned, and butchered about 4,280 buffalo in 18 months—a staggering number.

In the early 1870s, when some 2,000 buffalo hunters were camping on the Kansas range, frontier newspapers reported that the average marksman was downing 50 buffalo a day. Cody was credited with having killed twice that number on a good day.

Cody also gained notoriety and his nickname because of his attention-grabbing persona. He cut a dashing figure, with flowing blond hair and fringed buckskin outfits. He was also known as a swaggering braggart.

Cody scouted for the U.S. Cavalry in its campaigns against the Indians. He also guided buffalo hunts for the rich and famous, including publisher James Gordon Bennett and the Grand Duke Alexis of Russia.

In 1869, Edward Zane Carroll Judson, who under the name of Ned Buntline penned widely read "dime novels," traveled from New York to Kansas, searching for an authentic western hero for his next book. He met Buffalo Bill, and the American West was forever to be viewed in a different light. In ensuing years, Cody was the hero of 1,700 novels.

In 1872, Cody left the frontier, going to Chicago to star in the dramatization of Buntline's Buffalo Bill novel. He performed in the theater for the next 11 years, incorporating the mystery and majesty of the frontier into his Wild West Show. The show became an international success after appearing in London in 1887 for Queen Victoria's Jubilee. Buffalo Bill counted among his stars such famous names as Buck Taylor, Annie Oakley and Sitting Bull.

When the Wild West Show finally closed in the 1930s, Cody had traipsed around the world recreating spectacles of the western frontier—a Pony Express relay race, the holdup of a Deadwood stagecoach, Custer's last stand, and a variety of "cowboy fun" that later would become the stuff of rodeos. The show would never have been complete without Cody's own romanticized version of the buffalo hunt, a drama that could—and did—hold the audience spellbound.

The bison today

"In Montana, the trouble, as you know, was that we had buffalo, elk, deer, and a few sheep without making adequate arrangements for taking care of the surplus. Before it was realized, serious damage was done to forage, and it has had disastrous results." —American Bison Society

Ranchers played a major role in saving the bison. In the 1860s, they provided a sanctuary for the few remaining animals—both to avert extinction and to attempt to domesticate the wild bison and establish a breeding stock to mix with cattle.

In 1866, before the slaughter of the southern herds, Charles Goodnight captured three wild calves to establish a private herd in the Texas panhandle country. In 1873, Samuel Walking Coyote, starting with eight wild calves, began a herd in northwestern Montana. Descendants of the Walking Coyote herd, after becoming a part of the Pablo-Allard ranch herd, eventually were used to establish the National Bison Range at Moiese, Montana, in the early 1900s.

In 1881, at the height of the hunting of the northern herds, Frederick Dupree captured five buffalo calves in South Dakota. He maintained the purity of his herd, unlike the other early ranchers who routinely would crossbreed buffalo with cattle, yielding the "catallo." After Dupree died, James "Scotty" Philip purchased the herd, which grew to some 400 animals and later was used by the State of South

Dakota to establish the Custer State Park bison herd.

Sometime after 1886, Charles J. "Buffalo " Jones captured a number of calves, remnants of the southern herd, in the Texas panhandle. After trailing them to his ranch in Kansas, Jones acquired a group of bison bulls and cows from a Canadian herd in 1888. Jones used railroad stock cars to move the Canadian animals to Kansas, where the herd of about 150 was kept together until 1895. Jones initiated the practice of selling bison to zoos and parks, as well as to other individuals who wished to raise the animals.

These ranchers had made the first, and most important, move. They had preserved enough bison to let the federal government and the American Bison Society follow through with the lofty goal of creating ten national herds. Men such as Theodore Roosevelt and William T. Hornaday, the chief

Once nearly extinct, the plains bison now number about 100,000. Although bison had the evolutionary strengths to survive ice ages, diseases and predation, nothing prepared them for men with rifles.

taxidermist for the National Museum of the Smithsonian Institution, dedicated their efforts to preserving the bison as a wild species.

And they did it. By the 1930s, the group had been instrumental in establishing eight public bison herds and expanding the original stock of the private herds.

In 1905, private preserves and ranches owned 700 of the 800 surviving bison. The federal government controlled another 100, most of them at the National Zoological Park in Washington, D.C., and Yellowstone National Park in Wyoming.

From these survivors, the bison began its slow recovery. By 1907, the Wichita Mountains National Wildlife Refuge in Oklahoma had a small herd. In 1909, the National Bison Range near Moiese, Montana, started its herd. In 1913, Wind Cave National Park in South Dakota received a small herd of bison donated by the American Bison Society. The Fort Niobrara National Wildlife Refuge in Nebraska started its herd with a donation of six bison from rancher J.W. Gilbert and two from Yellowstone National Park.

These pioneering public herds marked the beginning of the federal government's efforts to bring the bison back. The public herds of today range in areas from small, fenced enclosures to the expansive highlands of Yellowstone National Park.

Yellowstone Park comes closest to what might be considered a complete ecosystem, and for the past 30 years bison have roamed free under the Park's "natural regulation" management policies. The smaller preserves have "enclave," or protected herds, sometimes existing in almost ranch-like conditions.

In attempting to recreate an original, nearly natural ecosystem, modern wildlife managers face limitations. Most

Lounging in the warm afternoon sun, a bison might lie flat on its side with its legs and head outstretched or on its belly with its legs tucked alongside or under its body. If especially lazy, it might even rest its head on the ground and close its eyes. But after about fifteen minutes, the bison must get up or risk accumulating fluid in its lungs, which can lead to pneumonia.

At the National Bison Range in Montana, the fourth successfully established public bison herd resides in this beautiful setting bounded on the east by the magnificent Mission Mountains.

notably, the public ranges generally do not include the numbers of natural predators that once followed the great bison herds. The grizzly bear and wolf have disappeared from the Great Plains and, with a few exceptions, from the foothills of the Rocky Mountains. Other predators such as coyotes and cougars still exist, but in reduced numbers.

Plus, the historic long migrations can obviously no longer occur. Today's public herds — even in Yellowstone Park — have manmade limits on their travel.

Each public bison herd has its own history, management style and unique attractions. And, of course, today's wildlife management must be innovative to come up with policy that strikes a fair compromise between modern civilization and the goal to create a wild habitat for the surviving bison.

Herds of bison on closed ranges must be inoculated against brucellosis and periodically thinned to protect the range against overgrazing. Excess animals are transplanted to other preserves or sold to ranchers.

As if on cue, two young bison make believers out of park visitors.

Yellowstone National Park

Observers of Yellowstone Park in the late 19th century, remembering the huge bison herds of recent history, had good reason to wish for a miracle to stave off extinction for the last wild herd of bison in the United States.

The wish came true. Today, Yellowstone has the largest public bison herd in the United States—and one of the wildest. In fact, this is the only bison herd that could be considered truly wild. The animals have lived in nearly natural conditions since the 1950s.

Historically, there have been four summer ranges and four winter ranges in Yellowstone. In summer, bison ranged north of Lamar, on the Upper Lamar-Mirror Plateau, in Hayden Valley, and on the Madison-Pitchstone plateaus. In winter, large herds moved onto the lower ranges of Lamar Valley in the north, as well as the Pelican, Hayden, and Firehole valleys to the south and west.

Today, the bison of Yellowstone have been returned to their historical ranges, grazing on grasses and sedges as they roam higher elevations in summer and descend to valleys and thermal areas in winter. As in the past, modern herds use the summer ranges scattered throughout the Park. Then, in the winter, the bison separate into distinct wintering

The central herd of Yellowstone National Park finds easy summertime grazing in Hayden Valley near the Yellowstone River, but they winter on the other side of Mary Mountain along the Firehole geothermal areas.

areas as they did in the past—the Lamar or northern herd of the Lamar Valley-Mirror Plateau region, the Pelican Valley herd, and the Mary Mountain herd, which crosses the mountain divide between Hayden Valley and the Firehole geothermal area.

The Yellowstone population reached its low point around 1900, when a count showed only about 25 wild bison remained in the Park. However, strong support came in short order from Congress and from private groups such as the Boone and Crockett Club. In fact, the early 1900s saw near-frantic efforts to preserve the bison and establish a captive herd in an atmosphere of inspired ranch management.

Even though Congress created Yellowstone Park in 1872, lawmakers failed to appropriate any money for management or protection of the Park until 1877. The civilian administration controlling the Park during these early years went unpaid and only visited the Park periodically. There were no laws, only vague rules and regulations that poachers knew were ineffective.

The U.S. Cavalry assumed jurisdiction of Yellowstone in 1886, beginning what would be a long and successful campaign to preserve bison in Yellowstone. With orders to "protect the buffalo," the Cavalry spent eight years fighting lawlessness and poaching. Then, finally, Congress stepped in to protect the natural treasures of Yellowstone, including the bison.

In 1894, just 13 days after Ed Howell, a notorious poacher, had been observed shooting and skinning five buffalo near Pelican Creek, Congress passed the Lacey Act. The law not only reinforced the nation's desire to preserve the last wild bison herd, it also provided Yellowstone with its first strand of enforcement power. After 1894, the Park could rely on the force of law, which in the case of killing bison meant a fine of up to $1,000 and up to two years in jail.

In 1894, the Smithsonian Institution tried to prod Congress into protecting wild bison with enclosures, but lawmakers balked at the expense. The next year, the Institution and the Cavalry did build an enclosure costing $3,000. A "stout fence of poles encompassing considerable area" was constructed on Alum Creek in Hayden Valley. Hay inside the fence was supposed to tempt the wild herd, and when enough bison had roamed inside, the Cavalry was to close the gates and begin to domesticate the animals. But a mild winter that year brought fewer bison than usual to the winter range, and the plan to capture bison here was unsuccessful, putting off for about ten years the idea of trapping Yellowstone's wild herd.

After the 1895 failure, Congress and the Cavalry decided capture of the wild herd was not possible. They redirected their efforts for the next seven years toward eliminating poaching and preparing plans to establish a tame herd by bringing more bison into the Park.

In 1902 Congress appropriated $15,000 to purchase eighteen bison cows—descendents of a herd owned by Samuel Walking Coyote and Charles Allard in Montana— and three bulls from the Goodnight herd in Texas. The Cavalry appointed "Buffalo" Jones as game warden. He stayed in the Park until 1905, when three years of political and

Along the oxbow bends of Trout Creek in Yellowstone Park, bison find nutritious, dense patches of sedges.

personal feuding with the Cavalry prompted him to resign and leave Yellowstone.

During his tenure, Jones built an enclosure for the new herd at what was then the Park's headquarters, Fort Yellowstone, near present-day Mammoth. At the same time, Jones built a smaller corral in Pelican Valley, so that he could capture wild calves to add to the new herd.

Range management, Yellowstone style, was in full swing by 1907. The captive herd at Fort Yellowstone had grown too large for the original enclosure, so it was moved to new pastures on Rose Creek in Lamar Valley. This "Buffalo Ranch" would remain a busy winter range until the 1950s.

Buffalo Ranch was aptly named. Corrals, barns, sheds, chutes, fenced pastures, runways, holding pens, and traps were all needed to manage the growing herd. Fields were plowed and planted with hay and oats.

The ranch crew handled the bison like cattle. They watched, guarded, and sheltered individual animals. To prevent injury, they separated cows and bulls on the winter range. They even removed calves from the company of cows.

In 1916, Congress transferred management of Yellowstone Park from the U.S. Cavalry to the National Park Service, but the Buffalo Ranch was still a busy place. A chief buffalo keeper and assistant, several herders, and an irrigator worked the ranch and range to keep the bison herd controlled and fed. Rangers from throughout the Park helped out with periodic roundups or reductions required to cull the population.

As much as 800 tons of supplementary hay, oats and other feed were required to feed the bison during some winters. In 1926 the winter range for the growing northern herd was expanded with the addition to Yellowstone of an

Despite their docile appearance, bison are extremely dangerous when approached too closely. They may charge with little provocation.

Top left: Bison frequently rub the bark from trees while using them for scratching and grooming hair and horns. Especially during the rut, trees take the brunt of bulls' aggressive actions.

Top right: In the midst of winter, the bison sweeps its head from side to side forming craters in the snow and uncovering last summer's grasses.

Left: When flies and other insects become unbearable, the bison wallows in the dust for relief. Snipe flies especially plague the bison in midsummer when its rear quarters have little protective hair. Bulls also use wallows to release some of their aggression—with no harm done.

area north of Gardiner, Montana. In the 1930s, the fences came down from around pastures, and the return to the open-range concept was begun.

Between 1907 and 1943, the Buffalo Ranch herd grew from 18 to 1,200 bison. Along the way, ranch managers removed about 2,625 animals, 700 of which were used to stock herds in other public preserves. The rest were butchered for meat in the Ranch slaughterhouse.

To be a ranger and work at Buffalo Ranch was a special privilege. But it also was hard work—not unlike working a cattle ranch. In addition to shielding the new bison herds from the dangers of disease and poor forage on winter ranges, the National Park Service also hunted predators because of their perceived threat to bison and other Park animals. The wolf disappeared, and other predator populations fell sharply.

The transition from ranch management to the regulation of free-ranging herds was triggered in the 1930s, when a study about the ecology of the coyote found that predator control harmed rather than helped herds of game animals, especially bison and elk. The predators served a purpose in the natural order, and the philosophy of non-interference with the ecological system was born.

For Buffalo Ranch, the change away from ranch management meant changing the face of the land. As the northern herd grew, rangers tore down fences, allowing the bison to roam farther into the mountains for summer range. By the 1940s—the last years of the Buffalo Ranch—intensive management waned, until even the autumn roundups and winter feeding ceased.

For nearly thirty years after 1907, Yellowstone supported two bison herds, the northern herd of about 1,200 animals centered at Buffalo Ranch in the Lamar Valley and the "protected" wild herd of some 150 animals in the Pelican Valley. The two herds maintained separate winter ranges, but on the open summer ranges they intermingled, blurring the genetic line between the original and introduced bison.

In 1936, rangers trucked a small herd of about 75 bison from Buffalo Ranch southwest into the Hayden and Firehole valleys in the central part of the Park. This re-established a herd on the last of the historical ranges for the first time since about 1895.

By the 1950s, when the ranch-management activities had been winding down for some 20 years until even feeding of winter hay was stopped, the total number of bison had increased to about 1,500, but the fortunes of the three herds were very different.

The northern herd in the mid-1950s numbered less than 300 animals, down from its peak of about 1,200 in the early 1940s. Meanwhile, the bison that were moved into Hayden Valley had expanded in range and number, becoming known as the Mary Mountain herd and growing to about 900 animals. The Pelican herd, the last herd of native Yellowstone bison, grew from about 25 animals in the early 1900s to between 100 and 200 from the 1920s to the 1940s. By the mid-1950s, the herd had grown to its peak of more than 450, but in 1957, following a severe winter and a decision by the Park Service to reduce the size of the herd, the Pelican herd dropped to fewer than 100 animals.

By 1966, a combination of severe winters and intentional removal had whittled down the total bison population in the Park from 1,500 to 300. Then rebuilding began again. Two easy years brought the population back up to 450, and numbers kept climbing to an all-time high of 2,200 in 1986. The Yellowstone bison herd is the largest to roam

Top: A cow nuzzles her 5-minute-old calf. Cows carry calves for nine months, usually giving birth in April or May.
Bottom: Half an hour old, the calf is ready to stand and nurse. The newborn weighs between 25 and 40 pounds.

Top: At one hour old, the calf tests its shaky, spindly legs while mother gives hers a rest.
Bottom: Within the first week of life, the calf is able to graze, drink water and gambol around its mother.

free in the United States since the early 1880s.

In the mid-1960s, the Park Service stopped controlling the herds. The Park Service converted bison management to a policy of natural regulation, which obviously didn't fit in with fences and corrals. Now, bison could live out their lives in as much "ecological completeness" as the Yellowstone ecosystem could provide. Thus, intensive management became minimal management. That meant, in part, that man could no longer feed or regulate the numbers of bison in Yellowstone.

By the 1980s, the bison herds had grown to more than 2,000 animals, and their historical ranges could no longer support them. As a result, the northern herd in the Lamar Valley, and to a lesser extent the Pelican and Mary Mountain herds, changed their patterns of grazing on both winter and summer ranges. The size of the herds and severe winters apparently pushed them into new grazing areas.

The Pelican and Mary Mountain herds began a small westerly expansion of their ranges, but they remained within the Park. The northern herd reacted more significantly. As early as the mid-1970s, the northern herd had begun exploring—and expanding into—new winter ranges, inside and outside the Park.

Although natural regulation is now the order of the day in Yellowstone, even the Park cannot provide totally natural conditions for its bison. For example, the wolf, perhaps the most efficient predator, no longer roams this area, and grizzly bears and cougars are not as plentiful as they once were. Some areas of the Park are not pristine, and many habitats are likely to change.

Finally, population growth and natural-regulation policies have influenced the behavior of the bison in Yellowstone, a trend that likely will continue.

National Bison Range

The National Bison Range at Moiese, Montana, is home to a public herd of bison established through the efforts of William T. Hornaday and the American Bison Society. It closely followed successes at the Wichita Mountains National Wildlife Refuge in Oklahoma and Yellowstone National Park.

From 1905 to 1907, Hornaday and the Society worked to convince Congress to purchase grassland in Oklahoma for the Wichita Mountains reserve. They also proposed a "buffalo refuge" on the Flathead Indian Reservation in Montana, land with a unique blend of mountains and grassland and conveniently located next door to the largest private herd of bison, the Michael Pablo herd, which numbered about 150 animals. President Theodore Roosevelt supported purchasing both the land and the Pablo herd.

In 1905, Congress rejected the first attempt to establish the National Bison Range, as lawmakers considered Pablo's asking price of $250 per animal too extravagant. Then, in 1906, Pablo sold his herd to the Canadian government for $200 per head, embarking on an epic six-year roundup at

Managers of the National Bison Range, near Moiese, Montana, stage a roundup every October to cull excess animals from the herd. Riders on horseback drive the animals into corrals, from which they are moved through a series of chutes. The roundup is open to viewing by the general public.

the end of which his original 150 buffalo had grown to 700.

When Pablo announced the sale of his herd to Canada, Congress became the target of criticism from an American public strongly supporting preservation of the bison. Lawmakers responded by appropriating $40,000 to purchase 18,542 acres of land from the Confederated Salish, Kootenai, and Pend d'Oreille tribes in 1908. By 1909 the land was fenced and ready to receive the nation's newest public bison herd, 37 animals in all.

As was the case in Yellowstone Park seven years before, 34 of these bison were descendants of the Samuel Walking Coyote herd. The family of Charles Allard had sold this group of bison to Charles Conrad, whose family in turn sold them to the National Bison Range.

Once again, placing bison on a protected range had been a collaborative effort of the federal government and the American Bison Society. The Society had raised more than $10,000 to buy the bison for $275 each. These bison, plus a few donated by various individuals, brought to 41 the number of animals populating the newest public reserve.

In 1909 there were 41 bison at the National Bison Range, 95 in Yellowstone Park, 20 in the Wichita Mountains in Oklahoma, and seven in the National Zoological Park in Washington, D.C.—a total of 163 animals.

The National Bison Range, commonly referred to as Moiese, features mountains covered with stands of ponderosa pine and Douglas fir. Valleys lined with aspen, cottonwood, birch, alder, and juniper trees cut through the foothills and open onto lush grasslands. The refuge still resembles the bison habitat of the 1800s. Bison graze on the open grassland and retire into sheltered, steep areas to rest among stands of forest.

During the nearly 80 years since the Bureau of Biological

Survey, the forerunner of the U.S. Fish and Wildlife Service, managed the Bison Range, the herd has increased to about 350. The U.S. Fish and Wildlife Service now controls the Bison Range, and management practices have changed.

To begin with, the Fish and Wildlife Service wanted other large hooved animals to share the National Bison Range. By the 1920s, elk, pronghorn antelope, bighorn sheep, mule deer, and white-tailed deer had joined the dominant bison. Meanwhile, the bison herd had grown to some 700 animals, along with 650 elk and hundreds of other big game animals.

As in Yellowstone Park, managers viewed predators as a mysterious threat, and they anxiously shot, trapped and poisoned them at every opportunity. But as the herds of bison and other animals grew unchecked by predators, their heavy grazing began to deplete the plant communities of the Bison Range. Faced with potential starvation of the entire bison herd, ranch managers adopted new practices in the mid-1920s, beginning with the hunting of game animals and supplemental feeding of hay.

By the 1930s, only 350 bison remained, and other game populations had also been reduced. Antelope had died out altogether. Watering ponds were built and supplemental feeding of hay continued, but despite controls, bison and other animals still kept overgrazing their habitat.

Faced with the terrible conditions of their range, the managers stopped the supplemental feeding, started annual autumn roundups, and divided the range into eight fenced pastures. By rotating small groups of bison among the pastures, they were able to let each range sit idle part of the time. The managers also limited the bison population to 350 and controlled other game populations (150 elk, 100 antelope, 50 bighorn sheep, 40 mountain goats, and 200 of each deer species) to make sure they didn't outgrow the Bison Range. Finally, in the 1950s, the National Bison Range began to recover its plant communities.

The roundup to cull the bison herd is a public event held during the first week of October. Riders on horseback gather the herds and drive them into corrals, where animals move from holding pens through a series of chutes. Managers check the bison for disease, and female calves are inoculated against brucellosis. Calves are branded, and between 50 and 100 bison are removed from the herd and sold at a sealed-bid auction. Excess animals from the Bison Range attract buyers who use the bison to restock and expand public and private herds throughout the country.

Visitors to the Bison Range can drive either a short loop road or a 19-mile loop tour route for excellent wildlife viewing throughout the spring, summer, and fall.

The National Bison Range is a replica, on a small scale, of the great free-ranging herds. The Bison Range actively manages its herd in an attempt to recreate a natural environment. In the wild, the bison herds were at the mercy of climatic and range conditions, as well as predation from man and animal. The fenced environment of the National Bison Range, as well as the other national parks and preserves with limited areas of bison range, substitutes man's intensive management for the management of nature.

In the early 1930s, when the Bison Range was damaged

Created by an act of Congress in 1908, the National Bison Range was designed specifically for the preservation of the bison. Now, ironically, the U.S. Fish and Wildlife Service, which controls the range, must carefully manage bison to avoid overpopulation and, in turn, habitat deterioration.

by overgrazing, the American Bison Society made this statement: "In Montana, the trouble, as you know, was that we had buffalo, elk, deer, and a few sheep without making adequate arrangements for taking care of the surplus. Before it was realized, serious damage was done to forage, and it had had disastrous results. Now the Buffalo is reduced to 320 head, a large number of elk have been removed, deer have escaped or been killed, and there are only 37 sheep."

Now, ironically, the numbers of bison and other game animals that the Society considered disastrous have been maintained through better management.

Custer State Park

South Dakota was the first state to buy bison for a game preserve. Just as William T. Hornaday and the American Bison Society pioneered the bison herds of the federal government, three South Dakota men—Pete Dupree, James "Scotty" Philip, and Peter Norbeck—established bison in South Dakota's largest state park. In fact, ever since he drove the first automobile across South Dakota to the Black Hills in 1905, Norbeck—first as a state senator, then as a governor, and finally as U.S. senator—considered Custer State Park his personal project.

In 1912, over 48,000 acres in the southern portion of the Black Hills were established as the Custer State Forest. A year later, a 700-acre block of land was fenced within the forest, forming the Custer State Game Preserve. That same year, park managers purchased and moved a herd of 24 elk into the preserve.

Prior to their near demise, bison had freely roamed the grasslands of the southern Black Hills. It therefore seemed appropriate that they be reestablished in the area. A bison herd was purchased and established in the game preserve in 1914. The original 36 animals were from Scotty Philip, who ran a "buffalo ranch" near Fort Pierre, South Dakota. Philip's herd of 500 had originally come from five wild calves captured in the early 1880s by Pete Dupree.

Under the guidance of South Dakota Governor Peter Norbeck, in 1919 Custer State Forest officially became Custer State Park. The park was not created solely for the preservation of the bison; within its borders was a unique collection of scenery and other wildlife.

The bison herd continued to grow, and by 1940, the herd was at a level of more than 1,500 animals. During that time, South Dakota started managing Custer State Park as a self-supporting state enterprise, selling bison and timber, as well as charging visitor fees. The park operated a "locker plant" from 1940 to 1974, supplying buffalo meat for private purchasers.

By the late 1950s, the Custer State Park herd had swollen to nearly 2,000 animals. As in other bison preserves, the range was beginning to be overgrazed. To help keep the herd size down, park managers built corrals and, in 1960, began annual roundups. The first auction, selling live bison to private parties, was held at Custer State Park in 1961.

Today, the park's 73,000 acres are managed to provide quality habitat for all wildlife, including bison. The Custer State Park bison herd ranges in size from about 900 animals overwinter, to 1,400 in the summer after the calves are born. The park still holds annual fall roundups. Surplus animals are sold at the live public auction in

November as well as at a spring delivery calf sale. Revenue from the sale of bison makes up a portion of the park's annual operating budget.

The free roaming herds of bison continue to be the main attraction in Custer State Park. The network of roads through the park is sure to provide visitors with access to the herds. Scenic drives such as the Wildlife Loop Road and the Iron Mountain Road offer some of the most dramatic views of bison in their natural Black Hills setting.

At Custer State Park in South Dakota, carefully planned management keep the bison herd at a desired level and age composition.

Badlands National Park

The 3,700 square miles of "badlands" in southwestern South Dakota have been described as an intricately adorned amphitheater, about the size of Yellowstone National Park.

Within the 382 square miles of Badlands National Park, there exists probably the largest intact prairie ecosystem in the United States. Mixed grasses grow in gently rolling valleys between spectacular formations of eroding sandstone, limestone, and other sedimentary rocks.

Badlands was first established as a national monument in 1939. However, until 1962, cattle grazed much of the range, limiting the number of big game animals. After 1962, the range began to recover and the value of its unique prairie ecosystem became more fully understood and appreciated. Congress redesignated Badlands as a national park in 1978.

Plains bison had disappeared from the range of the Badlands in the 1860s, some 20 years earlier than on other ranges. After an absence of more than a century, plains bison were reintroduced to the northern range at Badlands in 1964, creating the last major public herd.

In 1964 and 1965, about 30 bison were moved to Badlands from Theodore Roosevelt National Park in North Dakota and Fort Niobrara National Wildlife Refuge in Nebraska. By 1967, the herd had grown to more than 120, and then in 1987, to 450.

Badlands National Park is a blend of the old and new. The steep landforms of the badlands mix with wetlands of the White River and its tributaries to provide the backdrop for a history lesson of how the Indian tribes

After an absence of more than a century, plains bison were returned to the range at Badlands National Park in 1964.

hunted bison on the Great Plains. Bison grazing the water-shed of the White River were easy targets for the Indians. Arikara and Sioux traveled often through the area, fighting each other and hunting bison, often while on trading expeditions to the Black Hills.

Since before 1770, when the Sioux first began to use horses, bison were chased into contained areas lined with walls of rocks called "drift fences." There early roundups allowed Indians to shoot buffalo with bow and arrows at close quarters. Other times, hunters on foot or on horseback stampeded buffalo from along the banks of the White River, up into the maze of bluffs and over the cliffs.

Today, bison in Badlands National Park are often seen within a mile of those early buffalo jumps. Bison bones and Indian artifacts have been found at the bases of the buffalo jumps. Visitors are prohibited by law from removing these artifacts. The modern herd at Badlands grazes near Quinn Table and Roberts Prairie Dog Town along the Sage Creek plateau.

Lacking a limitless prairie to support its herd, the park controls the bison population by trapping cows, calves, and bulls, on the range where the herd grazes. These surplus bison are loaded into stock trucks and taken to the nearby Oglala Sioux Indian Reservation. The Oglala Sioux and the National Park Service are working to build the Oglala herd through the addition of Badlands surplus bison.

Wind Cave National Park

The bison herd at Wind Cave National Park was established in 1913, when the Wind Cave National Game Preserve received 14 bison from the American Bison Society. Six more animals were received from Yellowstone in 1916. Wind Cave was the last herd William T. Hornaday and the Society would stock in the West, although the preservation group continued to work with the federal government to build the herds until the 1930s.

With the arrival of the bison, Wind Cave, located in the southeastern corner of South Dakota's Black Hills, became "two parks in one." The park had been created in 1903 to preserve an outstanding limestone cavern. The third largest cave in the United States, it features extensive formations of limestone, "popcorn," "frostwork," and "boxwork." It winds through more than 45 miles of passages with cathedral ceilings. The boxwork formations are the most extensive of any in the known limestone caves of the world. At the entrance, a breeze rushes beneath an arch at velocities as great as 50 miles per hour, giving the cave its name.

Above ground, Wind Cave National Park contains approximately 44 square miles, 20 percent of them covered by ponderosa-pine forest and the remainder by prairie. Forested mountain ridges and rolling hills descend to mixed-grass prairie, with buffalo grass, grama grasses, wheatgrass, and bluestem grass.

The original Park contained 4,160 acres—about 6½ square miles. Two additions during its first 20 years increased the size of the Park to just over 18 square miles. At the same time, the Wind Cave bison herd grew to only 206 animals from the original 14. The first roundup in 1936 resulted in the removal of only three animals. By comparison, in the same amount of time, the bison herd at the National Bison Range in Montana grew from 41 to more than 700. In the Park's early years, domestic cattle competed with bison, helping keep bison numbers down. In 1939, however, the Park was limited to wild animals only.

The increase in acreage of Wind Cave National Park in its early years gradually increased areas of open range. By the mid-1930s the herd was able to move from winter to summer ranges, providing a natural rotation of forage with the change of seasons. Steady growth of the Wind Cave herd averted the early pattern of other preserves, where an exploding population resulted in overgrazing and then starvation.

In the 1940s, the Wind Cave herd started growing more rapidly. The Park was expanded to its present size of 44 square miles in 1946. In 1952, 173 animals had to be slaughtered to keep the herd below 300. The herd ballooned to 300 again in the 1960s and had to undergo another major cut—130 animals. The Wind Cave herd was now experiencing growth in 15 years that usually took 40 years.

By the mid-1970s, 60 years after 14 animals were turned loose on the range, the Wind Cave herd reached its peak of 560 bison. Through the mid-1980s, the herd has been cut to about 350 bison, with roundups every two years.

In the early sun, a herd of bison at Wind Cave National Park move toward a nearby prairie dog town.

Wind Cave keeps its bison herd at 350 on an open range that also supports 400 elk, 120 pronghorn antelope, 120 mule deer, and nine prairie dog towns. The sparse vegetation of prairie dog towns makes them ideal for wallowing, and they are used frequently by the herds during the summer breeding season.

An eight-foot, woven-wire fence encloses Wind Cave Park. The bison tend to stay in the open like plains bison, but at times they graze in smaller meadows, in the forested sections of the park. Cows, in particular, tend to favor these meadows during calving season. During harsh winters, the herd usually frequents the Red Valley. The rest of the year, and during mild winters, it ranges the entire park.

The bison roundup is generally conducted every other year. Through a cooperative agreement between the National Park Service and the Bureau of Indian Affairs, any surplus bison culled from the Wind Cave herds provide meat for Native American tribes.

Visitors to the Park will find excellent roadside viewing of the herds—especially in July and August near the prairie dog towns.

The bison and prairie dog—two species once incredibly abundant on the Great Plains—still exist in relative harmony at Wind Cave National Park. Bison and prairie dogs often share the range, to the benefit of both. As they graze, prairie dogs crop short the grasses surrounding the "town," thus encouraging new growth. Bison attracted by the tender, young shoots also find the bare, dusty center of the dog town an ideal place to wallow. The bison's trampling further contributes to long-term vegetation changes that promote expansion of the dog towns.

Like most wild animals, bison—such as the young bull—are more active at dawn than during the heat of the day.

The rutting season begins as early as the end of June and continues into September. This bull tries to urge a cow to her feet before a competitor can arrive to challenge his right to her.

Theodore Roosevelt National Park

Theodore Roosevelt National Park—in country known as the Little Missouri Badlands of western North Dakota—is a restoration project with a perspective perhaps more contemporary than that of some older parks and preserves. The Little Missouri River cuts through the Park's three units, which cover more than 100 square miles of the scenic North Dakota Badlands near the historic frontier town of Medora.

Established in 1947, the Park contains the site of the Elkhorn Ranch of Theodore Roosevelt—buffalo hunter, badlands rancher, respected naturalist, conservationist, and President of the United States. Situated along a remote stretch of the Little Missouri, the ranch site comprises the Elkhorn Ranch unit of the Park.

The range of the Park is varied. Rocky bluffs of scoria rock loom 650 feet above broad valley floors, and steep slopes, wooded ravines and draws provide a contrast to the cottonwood forests and grassland terraces. Open areas are spotted with prairie dog towns and sagebrush bottoms, while nearby waterways flow lazily along. The contrast of prairie and badlands evokes an appreciation for the powerful forces that created this land.

The territory covered by Theodore Roosevelt National Park was part of the range of plains bison in the 1800s. When bison herds were at their mightiest over the Great

Plains, prairie grasses grew at the whim of nature, influenced by rainfall, the scything migration of grazing animals, and the effects of prairie fires. White settlers on the Great Plains, and especially in the Little Missouri Badlands, altered the balance of nature. The buffalo, the supreme grazing animal, was wiped out, and fire suppression interfered with the normal growth and evolution of prairie plants.

The badlands became farm country in the early 20th century. Homesteaders prospered through the 1920s, right up to the Great Depression of the 1930s. Historians ruefully noted that the badlands had become "too thickly settled for every farmer to make a go of it."

Then the spectacular scenery of the badlands began to draw attention, ushering in yet another new age when bison, wild horses, bighorn sheep, white-tailed and mule deer, pronghorn antelope, and elk again would graze there.

Theodore Roosevelt became a national memorial park in 1947, three-quarters of a century after Yellowstone ushered in a "modern era of wildlife and wilderness preservation" as the nation's first national park. Buffalo would not graze its ranges until more than 50 years after Yellowstone began its preservation efforts at Buffalo Ranch. But bison returned to the badlands in 1956.

Today Theodore Roosevelt National Park has two bison herds—about 250 on the south unit and 120 on the north. There are no bison on the Elkhorn Ranch unit. Twenty bison were moved onto the north unit from the south in 1962. The 370 bison have grown from an original herd of 29 animals born on the Fort Niobrara Wildlife Refuge in Nebraska. The Park's bison may be hybrids of plains and mountain stock, a switch from the pureblood plains bison that roamed the badlands in the past.

In the rugged topography of Theodore Roosevelt National Park, bison find food on the ridgelines and tops of plateaus during winter. Photo by G.T. Altoff.

The two bison herds move freely within the fenced boundaries of the north and south units, sharing the range with wild horses and elk in the south. The bison are known to visit every area of the Park, but they most frequently graze along upland grasslands, old river terraces, and on the edges of prairie dog towns. They usually remain only briefly in the Park's lower reaches.

Although the two herds are counted annually, the National Park Service usually rounds them up every two or three years to inspect, vaccinate, and cull excess animals from the range. During the first 20 years that bison were in the Park, more than 1,000 animals were transferred to other public and private herds, with some 900 of those going to herds on Indian reservations. Before 1970, some buffalo from the Park were moved to zoos and other national and state parks, including Grand Teton National Park in Wyoming. Since about 1970, bison taken from the range have been trapped and shipped live to Indian tribes throughout the Great Plains states.

Excellent viewing opportunities are available to visitors who drive the Park's roads.

Bison seem harmless as they peacefully graze, but they can move with amazing quickness. Here, a trusting bird uses a grazing bison as a convenient perch.

Grand Teton National Park

The Snake River Valley in which Grand Teton National Park is located is one of the most dramatic in the Rocky Mountains. Twenty-five miles across and circled by mountains, it stretches southward from Yellowstone National Park for more than 50 miles. The jagged peaks of the Teton Range rise as a backdrop 7,000 feet above pine-forested slopes and a sagebrush-shrouded floor.

The history of the bison in Grand Teton parallels the fate of the animal elsewhere in North America. The earliest known large herd roamed the area east of the Snake River and 25 miles northwest of Jackson in 1833. But bison vanished from the area by 1840, about 60 years before the near-extinction of bison in Yellowstone. The bitter winters of the Rockies and increased hunting pressure certainly contributed to the early demise of the bison here.

Remains of these early bison have been discovered in areas of the Park that today, as in the past, provides the best winter range—along the Gros Ventre and Snake rivers, on the west slopes of the Gros Ventre Range, east across the Snake River, and in the Gros Ventre Valley, location of the National Elk Refuge. In summer, range was abundant along the east slopes of the Teton Range and west of the Snake River, where the re-established herd can be seen today.

After an absence of more than a century, bison were reintroduced to Grand Teton in 1948. Twenty animals were moved from Yellowstone to the Jackson Hole Wildlife Park near Moran, Wyoming. The Wildlife Park, 700 fenced acres, was built with money from the Rockefeller Foundation and operated as a private game preserve for 20 years.

For 15 years, the size of the herd fluctuated between 15 and 30 animals. Then, in 1963, an outbreak of disease necessitated the slaughter of all but four calves. The next year, 20 adult bison were shipped to the Grand Teton herd from Theodore Roosevelt National Park in North Dakota.

By 1968, the new herd had declined to 15 bison, all of which escaped from the Wildlife Park that summer. Six perished in the ensuing roundup, and another six were captured and returned to the range at Moran. But three bison eluded capture and moved south about 25 miles to the National Elk Refuge northeast of Jackson, Wyoming. At the Refuge, which provides supplemental winter feed, the Grand Teton bison mingled with an elk herd of as many as 7,000 animals.

In the spring of 1969, the fences were removed from around the Wildlife Park allowing bison to range freely throughout the Grand Teton-Jackson Hole area. The three errant bison returned from the Elk Refuge to the summer range, rejoining the larger herd. But they shared knowledge of their newfound winter range to the south, and the entire herd now makes the trek toward Jackson for the colder months.

By the mid-1980s, the bison herd grew to about 100 animals. It continues to summer in Grand Teton National Park and winter on the National Elk Refuge.

Trappers in the nearby Jackson Hole area may have been responsible for the early demise of bison on the east side of Grand Teton National Park. Photo by Franz J. Camenzind.

Wood Buffalo National Park

Wood Buffalo National Park in Canada has the largest herd of free-ranging bison in the world. Some 4,300 buffalo roam 17,300 square miles of subarctic terrain sprawling across Alberta and the Northwest Territories.

Wood Buffalo, with four times the land area of Yellowstone National Park, has been the last refuge in Canada not only for wild plains bison, but also for wood bison. The Park became the focal point of preservation after bison herds on Canada's western prairies and in the forests were decimated by hunters in the latter half of the 19th century.

The "great hunt" spilled across the U.S. border with Canada. For years, buffalo runners in Montana and Alberta depended upon the north-south seasonal traffic of the herds. In fact, the hunt was publicly deemed to have ended only after most of the last plains buffalo in the northern herd were chased from Montana into Canada sometime during the spring of 1882; the northern herd would never return.

While Canada had always been the range for millions of bison, by 1893 only about 250 survived in the far north. As in the United States, private ranchers protected small herds after the turn of the century. And the link between the wild herds of the United States and Canada continued, as buffalo in tame herds were purchased and transported back and forth across the border.

James McKay was the first Canadian to purchase buffalo and run them on fenced land. In the early 1870s, he bought six calves that had escaped "hide hunters," driving them from Alberta to his ranch in southern Manitoba. This first protected Canadian herd increased to 36 bison by 1880 when, after McKay's death, they were purchased by Colonel Sam Bedson and pastured with "good grass," still in Manitoba, on grounds outside the walls of the Stoney Mountain penitentiary.

Over the years, buffalo from this herd were spread far and wide. Early on, a number of animals were donated to zoological societies in New York and London. The American Bison Society would later come to depend upon the New York stock to help start new American herds. In 1887, the last 50 buffalo from the McKay-Bedson herd were sold to C.J. "Buffalo" Jones, who trailed and shipped them by rail to his ranch in Kansas. By the mid-1890s, Jones had turned these and his other bison over to Michael Pablo and Charles Allard, who used them to build the greatest herd of buffalo since the early 1880s.

The Pablo-Allard herd flourished on the wild range of the Flathead Valley in northwestern Montana until Allard died and Pablo failed to convince the U.S. Congress to buy his animals to start the National Bison Range. By 1907, twenty years after the remnants of the McKay-Bedson herd were shipped out of southern Manitoba, Pablo shipped back to Canada 709 bison, all of which were from plains stock. The returning herd headed into such preserves as Elk Island Park, Banff National Park, and Wood Buffalo National Park, the last Canadian province of the reclusive wood bison.

The Canadian preserves allowed bison herds to replenish in much the same way as the public herds in the United States. By 1920, Canada counted 1,500 bison in its herds. As the herds continued to grow throughout the first half of the 20th century, over 6,000 plains bison were transplanted into Wood Buffalo National Park alone; at the same time the number of native wood bison grew to 1,500 to 2,000.

Just as in Yellowstone National Park, where two different bloodlines of bison intermingled on summer ranges, large herds of plains bison mixed with smaller numbers of wood bison in Wood Buffalo National Park. New generations of hybrid animals eventually erased the bloodlines that might have distinguished the plains from the wood variety, so that by the 1950s Canadian wood bison were no longer believed to exist as a separate subspecies.

In 1959 a small herd of presumably pureblood wood bison was discovered in a remote, northwestern corner of Wood Buffalo. These animals may have remained untouched by outside forces over the centuries, mostly because the area they lived in was secluded and almost impossible to reach. The herd was captured and isolated near Fort Smith. In 1965, 23 of these bison were taken to Elk Island Park near Edmonton and 18 were sent to the MacKenzie Bison Sanctuary in the Northwest Territories near Fort Providence.

Today the Canadian Wildlife Service protects these last wood bison to ensure their continued existence. □

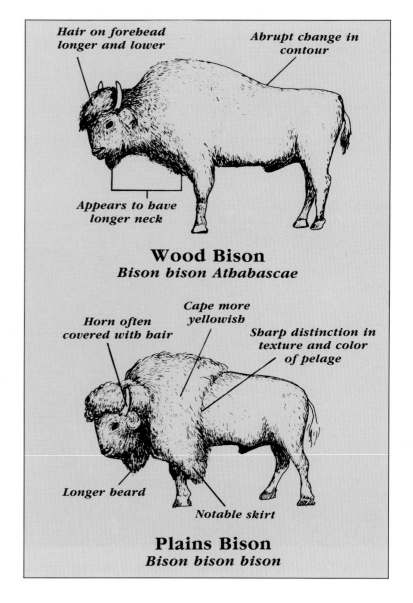

Hair on forehead longer and lower

Abrupt change in contour

Appears to have longer neck

Wood Bison
Bison bison Athabascae

Horn often covered with hair

Cape more yellowish

Sharp distinction in texture and color of pelage

Longer beard

Notable skirt

Plains Bison
Bison bison bison

A mature bull in the rut is much more active than normal—even at first light.

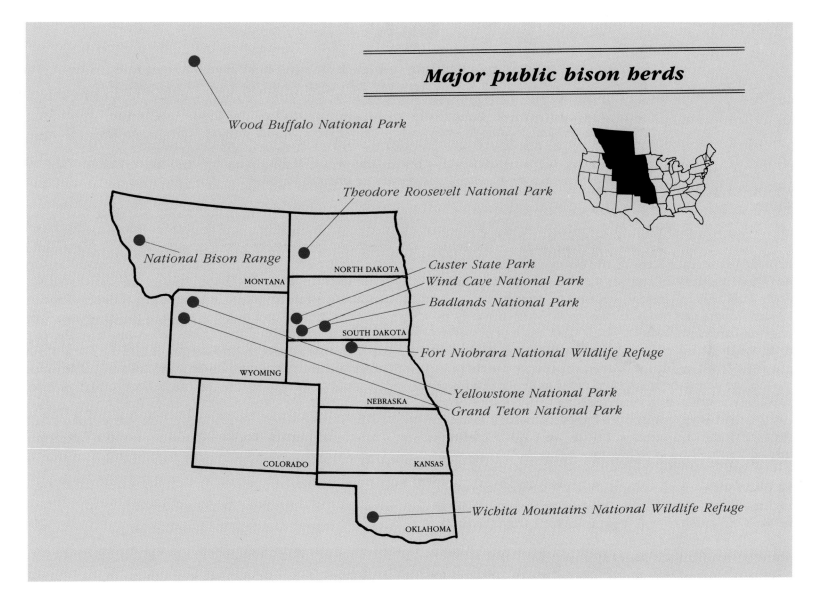

Major public bison herds

Wood Buffalo National Park

Theodore Roosevelt National Park

National Bison Range

NORTH DAKOTA

MONTANA

Custer State Park

Wind Cave National Park

Badlands National Park

SOUTH DAKOTA

Fort Niobrara National Wildlife Refuge

WYOMING

Yellowstone National Park

NEBRASKA

Grand Teton National Park

COLORADO

KANSAS

Wichita Mountains National Wildlife Refuge

OKLAHOMA

The bison tomorrow

"The hunter usually waited until afternoon when the small herds were returning from water and were lying down to rest. He would then creep up on the herd from the leeward side and take his position. The leader was usually the one to be shot first. The other buffalo would mill around their fallen leader, not knowing what to do. The hunter would then shoot those animals tending to stray away from the herd. In this way the hunter could kill as high as one hundred animals in one hour. The whole herd might be slaughtered in several hours, but more often one of the animals would become panic-stricken and break away from the herd, causing the remaining animals to follow." —Gary Eichhorn

Thanks in part to a last minute, dramatic conservation effort, the bison continues to roam the face of the earth. Humans, who almost were responsible for its annihilation, instead became its rescuers.

Many Americans today do not realize the bison is no longer endangered. Roughly 100,000 strong, it grazes safely in national parks, preserves, reservations, and wildlife refuges, as well as (not so safely) on private ranches.

In an age when the media and environmental groups so constantly announce the approaching extinction of other species, the bison represents a happy comeback story. In all fairness, the conservation efforts were not the bison's only salvation. Bison in Yellowstone National Park and what is now Wood Buffalo National Park were so remote that the bison there escaped the fate of their more accessible brethren on the Great Plains. But dedicated people all over the West did much to pull the species back from the brink. Today, other dedicated people work to safeguard the bison's future on remnants of its former ranges.

Perhaps the best way to fully appreciate the bison is to seek out a herd sometime in the latter half of the summer, the time of the rut, the peak of activity on the bison's calendar. An observer soon senses the power of this enduring creature, not only in its physical dimensions and actions, but also as a living symbol of the American West.

With a little imagination, one can conjure up the days of the buffalo hunters, buffalo jumps and the Great Plains unfenced and black with bison for miles around. Push the imagination a bit more, through thousands of bison generations, ice ages, saber-toothed tigers, the crossing of the Bering Strait Land Bridge, back to the Asian cradle of early mammals. Today's bison stands as a fascinating chapter in the book of Earth's natural history. □

During the rut, the spectacular clashes between bulls stem more from a desire to prove superior strength and size than from a dispute over which bull will pair with which cow. This herd of bison grazes peacefully at Custer State Park, enjoying a lull between these "fighting storms."

Major public herds

Yellowstone National Park, Wyoming
   3,472 square miles, 2,500 bison.

National Bison Range, Moiese, Montana
   29 square miles, 300-350 bison, plains bison
   herd established in 1909.

Wind Cave National Park,
 Hot Springs, South Dakota
   44 square miles, 350 bison, plains bison herd
   established in 1912.

Custer State Park, Custer, South Dakota
   113 square miles, 900 bison, plains bison
   herd established in 1914.

Badlands National Park, Interior, South Dakota
   382 square miles with north and south units,
   450 bison on north unit, park managers
   considering establishing herd on south unit in
   cooperation with Oglala Sioux Tribe, plains
   bison herd established in 1964.

Theodore Roosevelt National Park,
 Medora, North Dakota
   108 square miles on north, south, and Elkhorn
   Ranch units, 120 bison on north unit, 250 bison
   on south unit, none on ranch unit, plains bison
   herd established in 1956.

Grand Teton National Park, Moran, Wyoming
   1,250 square miles, 100 bison, plains bison herd
   established in 1948.

Fort Niobrara National Wildlife Refuge,
 Valentine, Nebraska
   30 square miles, 300 bison, plains bison herd
   established in 1913.

Wichita Mountains National Wildlife Refuge,
 Indiahoma, Oklahoma
   35 square miles, 600-700 bison, plains bison herd
   established in 1907.

Wood Buffalo National Park, Alberta and
 the Northwest Territories, Canada
   17,300 square miles, 4,300 wood-plains bison
   established in 1922.

Suggested Readings

Cates, Jon, 1986, *Home on the Range, The Story of the National Bison Range.*

Dary, David, 1974, *The Buffalo Book.*

Meagher, Mary, June 16, 1986, *"Bison bison, Mammalian Species."*

McDonald, Jerry N., 1981, *North American Bison: Their Classification and Evolution.*

McHugh, T., 1972, *The Time of the Buffalo.*

Sandoz, Mari, 1954, *The Buffalo Hunters.*

Seton, E.T., 1929, *Lives of Game Animals, (Part two).*

In addition to these books, two national groups which publish periodicals with information on bison are:

National Buffalo Association
P.O. Box 706
Custer, SD 57730

American Buffalo Association
P.O. Box 965
Cody, WY 82414

Author's note: *Many able people helped bring this book project to a successful conclusion. To them I wish to express my appreciation.*

W. Perry Conway, Terry Hammell, G.T. Altoff, Franz J. Camenzind and Mary Meagher each generously allowed me to use one of their photographs to fill in the inevitable gaps of my stock.

John Hodnik researched a substantial portion of the material and interviewed several key sources of information.

The following people were immeasurably helpful in providing the facts and reviewing early drafts of the manuscript: John Malcom, Micki Hellickson, Bill Swift, Rich Klukas, Kay Rohde, Ernest Ortega, Dave McGinnis, Ron Green, Gene Ball, Sharlene Milligan, Don Haisman, Ken Walker, and Bob Lewis.

For her patience, inspiration, warm interest and many insights, I am especially indebted to Mary Meagher.

Thanks also to the Falcon Press staff, in particular Bill Schneider, Gayle Shirley and Jeri Walton, for their great work and encouragement.

And lastly, I can only hope that my wife Barbara knows my gratitude for her unstinting support and understanding.